HOW TO BE A

CW00495448

Learn the inside *secrets* for s   **sle**
on your luxury cruise with tl   **a**
"veteran" cruise๋ ๋฿ฑ๗ uver 27 cruises
to places as far apart as St. Petersburg and New York; Cairo
and the Caribbean; Africa and the Canary Isles.

By Dave Dutton

CONTENTS

"As a veteran of two cruises, I thought that I knew the ropes but this short ebook tells me in a humorous and insightful manner how to save money and add to the enjoyment. The `tricks of the trade` are outlined and several times I said to myself "why didn't I think of that?". If you are going cruising, it makes sense to take advice from a veteran of some 27 trips. A good read, and an invaluable tool." – Amazon reviewer.

Ready? Strike up the band and let's sail…

BOOKING TIPS

There's nothing guaranteed to ruin your cruise more than a noisy cabin. On almost every ship, there are "problem cabins" which are under gymnasiums; pools; theatres; restaurants or buffets and next to lifts or crew service areas. Avoid these like the plague. Look in the brochure and for peace of mind choose one that has cabins above, cabins below and cabins either side or as close as you can get to that. Some message boards and forums have lists of problem cabins and you would do well to take note of them. On one of our earlier cruises, we once booked a cabin which was under the buffet area of the Aurora and from very early to very late, the trolleys being wheeled overhead sounded like thunder. It was difficult to get proper sleep and the cruise was a long one to Egypt as well! Lessons are learned the hard way. *Make sure you learn from our experience.*

Some cruise agencies book blocks of cabins and it's usually cheaper to book through them than the cruise operator themselves and sometimes have availability when the operator's website is showing fully booked. It's worth checking.

Some balcony cabins can be looked down on from above. If you're planning a spot of nude sunbathing, check with your TA (Travel Agent) for the best option.

If you are going on a cruise for some much needed sunshine, consider Freedom Dining (or the equivalent) or second sitting. It will give you time to relax by the pool after a day ashore and there will definitely be no shortage of sun loungers available.

If you're a bad traveller or get queasy easily, go for a cabin amidships and low down. You'll suffer less from the effects of bad weather or ocean conditions.

If you can afford it and you can take the risk, you can buy stocks and shares in some cruise lines and as well as getting the dividends, you can get generous OBC (onboard credit) for your cruise, as long as you let the company know beforehand. This is set against what you spend on the cruise, so be sure you spend it all as it is non-refundable.

Bargains can be had if your circumstances allow you to book at the last minute. The downside is that you won't have much choice of cabin and it may be near the fore or aft of the ship. We once booked 3 days before sailing and got a 14 night Med cruise with P and O for £599 each – virtually half the advertised price – but the cabin was nearer the front of the ship than we would have liked. If you are on a budget, it's a chance worth taking. The cruise was fine though and we ate the same food and saw the same shows and ports as the folks who had paid double that amount.

You can also get bargains by booking nearer the time on a "guarantee cabin" basis. This is means you have no choice where it is situated, but may get an upgrade (but probably not) – although we once did this on a Canaries cruise and were upgraded from an inside to a balcony cabin. So it's pot luck really but for all our many cruises with P and O, this is the only time they've ever given us an upgrade. From a loyalty aspect, this is a source of a lot of frustration with many "veteran" cruisers but hey-ho. It varies between cruise companies as to when you will be informed which cabin you have been given, from weeks before to the day before.

Unless you're claustrophobic, an inside cabin is fine. You'll have more money to spend onboard or on other cruises and you'll sleep or nap better as it's almost pitch black when you switch the lights off. The ship will rock you to sleep like a baby. (Mini-tip– going back to the cabin for "a little lie down" after dinner will almost certainly result in you dropping off for the rest of the evening.)

When booking, specify your special dietary requirements if you have them. Whether they are vegetarian, vegan, gluten-free, diabetic or religion-based, your needs will be catered for.

Attention to detail is such that you can even specify beforehand how you want the bed arrangements – twin or king-size.

Parking services area available at the port of embarkation but these can be very costly – at present around £140 for a 14 night cruise. *You can usually find a hotel for less than that where you can stay at the night before you sail which will also allow you to park free for the cruise and sometimes even provide a shuttle to the ship.* We even stayed at a guest house once that did just that and we made considerable savings as well as enjoying an extra night's holiday.

Consider travelling by coach instead of driving. You will arrive less fraught and when you put your luggage on the coach, the next time see it will be outside your cabin.

Shop around for your cruise. Get a paper and pen and surf the various cruise agency sites. Don't just pay the first quote. You'll be surprised at the variation in cost and OBC (onboard credit).

When you get a quote, go to another TA and ask them for a quote. If it's more than the one you were originally quoted, tell them and more often than not, they will undercut that price.

Always book with a TA who is ABTA registered. We booked a cruise and the TA went bust but P and O took over the booking and handled it perfectly for us in conjunction with ABTA.

Some cruise lines allow you to put a deposit on a future cruise onboard, then give you generous onboard credit just for doing that. You can still go to any TA to fulfill the booking.

The best source of information regarding specific ships, cruise lines or destinations comes from those who have travelled before you. Forums are packed with information and your fellow cruising enthusiasts are always more than keen to show off their knowledge. Ask. Ask. Ask. Someone will know the answer and it will save you a lot of time and money. They know the best places to eat ashore; the cabins to avoid; the best taxi drivers to book; the good and the bad of various ships. They are a helpful lot and some even use the forums to arrange a meetup on a specific cruise. Cruise Critic, We Love Cruising and the cruise line's own forums are a good source of information and help.

CRUISIN' and BOOZIN' TIPS

If you haven't cruised before, you may be surprised to know that you can get free booze onboard your cruise. Provided you're the right age of course. There is generally a **"Welcome Aboard"** reception a day or so into the cruise at which you'll have the chance to have a glass or three of wine; a refreshing Gin and Tonic; A Whisky and Soda or soft drinks. There's nothing to stop you having several glasses and a lot of passengers take the drink in to dinner. Similarly at the Captain's Gala Reception, there is another chance to sample freebies, so if you're that way inclined, make the most of it!

Once you reach a certain level in the rewards scheme, there sometimes is a special lunch at which free drinks are served as well. These are very convivial events with an officer heading the table (and the Captain as well) and worth attending for the company and the free drink.

If you like to drink alcohol and intend bringing your own onboard, you'll have to check what that cruise operator's policy is because some don't allow it and will confiscate your precious bottles of whatever. Many cruisers have found ingenious methods of circumventing these restrictions (let's face it, Gin and Vodka look like water) and there is a thriving online trade in **"Rum Runner"** flasks which are made specially for smuggling booze onboard. They are collapsible, durable, reusable, undetectable and non-metallic. At the time of writing P and O allow you to bring your own drink onboard for consumption in the cabin.

When onboard, beware of **"upselling".** This is the practice by a waiter (on commission) of trying to make you spend more money and attempting to influence your choice of drink by asking if you want a certain brand (usually the most expensive) or asking if you want doubles. This may be done when you are in a group of friends and the waiter is relying on you not wanting to look a cheapskate by going for singles or the cheapest spirit on offer. Look at the drinks list beforehand and specify immediately the brand you want. On one cruise we did, the waiter kept insisting we have doubles and a quiet word was had with the bar manager.

"Cocktail of the Day" is sold cheaper than the normal price and can be a bargain – especially when there are several spirits included in the drink. Sometimes after dinner, the wine waiter will come round with post-prandial spirits or liqueurs at a vastly reduced cost.

Be aware that the champagne that the waiters hand out at sailaways is usually chargeable. You can, however, get free champers (well that's what they claim it is) at the art auction. Just make sure you don't consume too much of the stuff and make a rash bid on something you might later regret buying. Take the champers and run!

If you have the brass neck, there's nothing to stop you taking a glass of your own wine to dinner – after all, it looks like one you may have bought in a bar to finish off with your meal. You may be thought a cheapskate if anyone finds out though!

If you are a heavy drinker on a budget, it's probably best to avoid those cruise lines that automatically add as much as 15% mandatory service charge to every drink or bottle of wine that you buy. You'll get a nasty shock at the end of the cruise as the booze bill mounts up. Your TA will advise – (or read the small print in the brochure.)

EQUIPMENT TIPS

Based on personal experience, these are some suggestions about useful equipment you might like to take on your cruise.

Earplugs. There is the chance of noise pollution on a ship and that may interfere with you having a good time. Creaky cabins; noisy neighbours; crew moving stuff about early and later; loo-flushing; air-conditioning; waves against the side of the ship and being too near the inner workings of the ship or the entertainment areas are just some of the possible problem areas. Your earplugs will go a long way to making sure you have a good night's sleep or nap. The gel ones or the ones made of foam are the best to use. The wax ones tend to be a little uncomfortable. Experiment at home with them a few days before you travel to see which suit you best.

Mini First Aid Kit. Because accidents or overindulging happens, it's as well to be prepared with a few items such as plasters; antihistamine cream (insect bites) ; indigestion tablets; hangover relief; antiseptic cream; your preferred pain relief tablets; witch hazel for bruises; bandages and diarrhoea medication – just in case you get a dodgy meal onshore.

Vitamins. The main ones being Vitamin C and Milk Thistle to be taken after one of the many boozy sessions you might find yourself inadvertently being involved in. They help process the alcohol to make it less harmless and also help the liver. (Check first that these are suitable for you).

Antibacterial handwash and hand sanitisers. Without wishing to scare you or make you paranoid, I would strongly advise you to definitely include these in your essential equipment. Use them frequently onboard and ashore. I have been on cruises where the hand gel wasn't brought into use before it was too late and the norovirus started affecting some passengers. It's a closed environment and some people aren't as fussy as you about hand washing after they've been to the lavatory. Safety first. You'll be glad you brought them.

Sunscreen\ After Sun Lotion\ Lip Balm Don't fall victim to "Lobsteritis" as I call it. At the first suggestion of sunshine, people lie out far too long without realizing how strongly the sun affects your skin on a ship. The cooling breeze is very deceptive. I guarantee on a sunny cruise that within the first couple of days, you'll barely be able to suppress a snigger at the guys who come down to dinner in a tuxedo\ dinner suit with a face like a tomato. You'll see them on the picture gallery as well. Always good for a laugh. Just make sure that you're not the one being laughed at.

Muscle spray. If you're prone to cramp or various aches and pains, pack one of these. You'll probably be dancing; using the gym and walking long distances ashore which can bring on an attack of cramp. It's happened to me a couple of times. The first time was on my very first cruise when a painful episode of cramp badly affected my right calf on the morning I was due to drive 200 miles home! I went to the medical bay and asked if they would be so kind as to spray it for me. They said they *would* be so kind, but would charge me £25 for the pleasure. I voiced my opinion on the matter; hobbled off the ship; bought some ashore and drove gingerly home.

Seasickness Tablets. I've never been seasick. I don't believe in it! I've been in a Force 11 and it didn't affect me. I guess I'm one of the lucky ones. Many aren't. So it may pay you to bring some medication onboard with you although some people swear by acupressure wristbands or ginger to quell the nausea. Whatever works for you.

A Corkscrew \ Bottle Opener. No need to tell you why.

Coffee\ Teabags. This may sound strange but you may prefer your usual brand to the ones onboard in your cabin. Put some in a plastic bag or a small Tupperware type container and pop it in your case.

Folding Nylon Rucksack. Useful for bringing stuff to and from your ports of call.

Extension Sockets \Double Adaptor\Power Strips Some cabins don't have enough sockets for your to charge your smartphone or work at your computer while your wife dries her hair. This will save arguing over who has custody of the socket.

Travel Adaptor. If you're from the UK and going on an American cruise ship, you will probably need one of these to convert from a UK 3 pin to a US 2 pin. Likewise, the other way round.

Small pair of binoculars. *"What's that liner over there?"* *"Dunno. Too far away to see."* Stash a small pair away and you'll be glad you did. You'll also need them for close-ups of those wonderful dolphins which are often to be seen at sea or swimming alongside the ship.

Insect repellent. Because no-one wants to get a nasty bite on their holidays.

Photocopies of your passport and travel\health insurance. In case the worst happens.

Bank and credit card company emergency numbers. So you can stop your cards in case they get stolen ashore. Also inform your credit card company you will be going abroad or they may stop your card thinking it's a suspicious transaction.

Torch\ Flashlight. Handy in an emergency but also useful for those middle-of-the-night toilet trips.

Extra pair of glasses. I once broke mine on a cruise and had to squint at menus. Thankfully, it was towards the end of the holiday.

Trousers and skirts with elasticated waistbands for longer cruises. Seriously! It goes without saying that you will be eating a lot more than you normally do and if on a longish cruise (or even a shortish one depending how much you eat) you will need clothes you can actually fit into.

Deep conditioner for your hair as the sea and sun can quickly dry your hair up.

Spare batteries and SD cards for your camera. Also, all the leads you need for your gadgets.

Lengths of thick elastic bands. These will come in surprisingly handy for securing the towels you lie upon on your sunbed or lounger as it's naturally breezy on the open decks and these will stop them flapping about or blowing away. Don't bring any beach towels. All towels are provided.

Light thermal mug. Useful for taking chilled or hot drinks ashore (especially if the local water is dodgy) and fiendishly useful as a disguise for keeping chilled white wine in by the pool if you want people to think you are simply sipping tea!

Highlighter pen. When you get the "What's On" paper in your cabin outlining the next day's social events or activities, you can highlight the ones you fancy for easy reference the following day. Also useful for noting important information regarding ports; emergency numbers; disembarkation times etc.

Over the door shoe organizer. This can be used in the bathroom to store your toiletries and any personal bathroom items you may have brought with you.

ONBOARD MUST DO'S (AND DON'T'S)

If your cases are taking up too much room in your cabin, ask your steward to stow them away for you. Sometimes, they will also store under your bed. If you decide to leave your suitcases in the cabin you can use them to store clothes that won't crease: such as socks and underpants etc.

To help with orientation, when you come out of a lift on your particular deck, have a look at which picture or artwork is on the side of the corridor for your cabin. That way, you'll always remember it's right rather than left (or vice versa). The colour of the carpeting usually is significant in matters of direction. Check where the different colours lead.

If you want to book a spa session, book early but be warned: they are expensive. If you want to pay a little less, look out for the special offers on port days when most people will be ashore.

If you are an avid reader, make a beeline for the library as soon as it's open when you get aboard.! The best books go first.

You don't have to go to all the port lectures or special activity events if you'd rather sunbathe or chill with friends as these are usually filmed and repeated many times on your cabin television.

Don't bother buying the cruise video. It's expensive and you'll probably only be on it for a split second waving drunkenly at the camera. When you get home, you will probably only watch it once or bore the backsides off friends and neighbours with it. Do yourself and them a favour and save your money.

Avoid buying the expensive photographs that will be taken of you at mealtimes. You'll probably have your digital camera with you and most ships offer a do-it-yourself printing service and show you how to work it. You will save a lot of money.

Avoid the Art Auction. General consensus is the pictures aren't as much of a bargain as they are made out to be and it's easy to get carried away by auction fever (or the free so called champers). You will probably see the same "works of art" time and time again every time you take a cruise. Some people have also claim to have never received the stuff they paid for.

Stay out of the casino or at least limit yourself to a small budget. Rumour has it that the slots always pay out well on the first day of a cruise to entice you to lose on the rest of the trip. I don't know how true this is but if enough passengers say it, it must be right! Also, when you've had a few drinks, you are more likely to get "suckered" into playing the tables then when you are sober. If that's your bag, go for it but otherwise go for a walk on deck.

Save money by **NOT** going on the ship's shore excursions. You will get the frighteners put on you by being told that if you make your own way ashore sightseeing, the ship won't wait for you if you are late or there are strikes on public transport. It could happen but generally speaking, you will save a massive amount of money by opting to go your own way. Get your dining companions to share a taxi or a minibus and you can see the same sights (and usually more interesting ones) at a fraction of the cost. There are always local taxis waiting by the ship and you can agree a price with the knowledgeable local driver. We have had some fabulous sightseeing tours this way. (*If you are ever going to Athens, google George the Famous Taxi Driver for a case in point. He got 4 of us safely back to the ship after some of the worst floods in the city's history when the rest of Athens ground to a halt).*

If you are going for fixed dining times, opt for the biggest table you can. If there are 8 people on the table, you are more likely to meet someone you get on with rather than on one with fewer diners.

If you have a special diet such as vegetarian or vegan, hopefully you will have noted that down on your booking form. There will always be a choice of food on that day's set menu but what some people don't realize is that there is usually a list of alternative choices that you can pre-book for the following day's meals! Having been informed of your preferences, the Maitre'd will come to you with the following day's menus and should you not like the choices available, will present you with a list (usually changed weekly) of starters; main courses and puddings from which you can choose. Now **THAT** is service.

As cruise lines tighten their budgets, sometimes staff find themselves coping with more passengers. It may take a while for the wine waiter to get to your table. A way round this is to order (if available and it usually is) a wine package. This is usually six bottles of really good wine sold at a discount and you let the waiter know which one you want for the following day. Owing to the fact the wine waiter has been given prior notice, the bottle will usually be waiting for you on the table when you arrive for your meal.

You don't have to drink all your wine in one go. The waiter will recork it for you and make a note of your table number. Even if you are on Freedom Dining, a note will be made of your name and cabin number and you can start off where you finished the night before.

You will pay a premium for meals at the specialty restaurants which have cropped up onboard in recent years. You will receive special service and the food is usually superb. If you are after a treat, go for it but my tip is to look out for special deals as soon as you board the ship. Sometimes, as a "taster" you will get the offers at a reduced price but book right away as these won't last long.

On the grounds that pence mount into pounds and dimes into dollars, you can save on buying bottled water by buying a couple ashore. In some continental supermarkets, it's a tenth of the price as the ones sold onboard.

If you *really* want to play bingo, wait until the last day when the jackpot is usually at its biggest and has to be won. You won't be popular with the regular players who seem to have an unerring nose for who hasn't been playing throughout the cruise but that won't worry you if it clears your onboard account – and with some to spare. It's usually in four figures.

Healthwise, I avoid touching the staircase rail with my bare hands if at all possible – especially if there is an outbreak of norovirus onboard. I realize this will be difficult for lots of people and I am **NOT** suggesting that you do the same but it makes me cringe when I see people running their hands all the way down the rail. When you think of all the people who have touched that rail before you: people who may not have washed their hands after using the loo or people with colds; it makes sense to have as little contact as possible with that bare surface. In a lift, I always use my knuckle to quickly tap the floor button. If this seems excessive, let me say that we were on the fated Aurora cruise on which the virus took hold and became world news. People were falling like flies. I said to a friend, "Don't touch the rail if you can avoid it". He did. He got the bug and was ill for days. I'm not saying he wouldn't have got it if he hadn't touched the rail but my wife and I didn't and we were fine. Don't worry though. Most cruises are trouble free. It's just something to bear in mind.

You don't really need to bring aftershave or perfume on the ship. The shops stocks most leading brand and you can dab some on whilst on your way down to dinner.

Sometimes large bottles of spirits and packs of cigarettes can be cheaper to buy onboard than ashore. Keep an eye open for special offers.

Learn a few words of whatever language your table waiters speak: such as " Thank You", "Please" and "Goodnight". I've picked up a few words of Hindi and Filipino from the crew and their faces light up when you make that small effort and they go out of their way to help you.

If using your cellphone as an alarm, remember to switch of data roaming to avoid hefty charges abroad.

On the last night of the cruise, take the hangers out of the wardrobes and put them somewhere under a cushion. Because there won't be any clothes on them, they will bang together and sound like the Bells of St. Mary's all night.

AVOID! (WHO AND WHAT)

Most people you meet on a cruise are just like you. All they want is a bit of rest and recreation and a chance to relax, have fun and make new friends. That is what usually happens. In fact I would go so far as to say that talking to people and people watching is one of the great pleasures of going on a cruise.

You never know who you are going to meet. You may bump into someone famous who is taking time out to enjoy themselves or you may meet someone so memorable, the time you spend with them becomes something you value for a long time..

Amongst the latter was a man who sitting with his wife on the next table to us at dinner. We noticed they weren't speaking much and thought they had fallen out but it turned out that he had Muscular Dystrophy and we eventually got talking and became great friends. He'd been a fireman and despite his many difficulties he had a twinkle in his eyes and was a joy to be with. Sadly, it was his last holiday as he died shortly afterwards but he will always be remembered by us.

You will meet people from other countries and other cultures: old and young alike. On longer cruises, camaraderie develops and you can't wait to all meet up.

But you get the odd one or two who are determined not to have a good time. **The Moaning Minnies**. Here is how you can usually spot them…

Avoid the following people.

They generally sit next to you uninvited or perhaps at breakfast and will almost certainly ask the following question…

"What do you think of the ship?"

A klaxon should sound in your head and you should get the heck out of there ASAP for what they really want to do is tell you what *they* think of the ship and it's usually not favourable.

We have been on some fabulous ships which anyone would normally be really grateful to have the chance to travel on but we have encountered these Moaning Minnies who, once they have cornered you, proceed to criticize everything about the ship from the décor to the carpets; from the crew to the standard of the food which on one memorable occasion included the comment *"The bacon on here isn't as crisp as it is on the Oriana"*.

Another question you should never respond to is...

"How much did you pay for this cruise?"

Uh Oh! That's a no-no. If you paid half what they did, they will be scandalized and give you an earbashing but if they paid half of what you did, they'll delight in telling you all about it and what great deals So and So Cruise Agency always give them – indeed they are on first name terms with the boss there.

What *not* to say – the following won't apply to you, obviously, as you have a lot more sense and taste.

Avoid calling the ship a boat (unless you want to wind someone up, of course). They'll go into great detail telling you what constitutes a boat as opposed to a ship. I did know once but I'm delighted to say I forgot. They will also tell you that you can put a boat on a ship but you can't put a ship on a boat. Yawn.

Avoid asking the Captain **"Who's driving the ship?"** if you see him doing his daily rounds. Chances are he has probably heard that 5,000 times before and feels like chucking you over the side.

Avoid referring to **"the sharp end"** and **"the blunt end"** of the ship. You'll be labelled as a cruise bore.

Avoid saying **"Well, we're on our way home now"** as soon as the ship heads homewards – even if it's as far away as Port Said. People don't like to be reminded of that.

Avoid saying to the "ethnic" waiters: **"I'm nearly as brown as you now"** if you've been out in the sun. Believe it or not, there are people like that and I've heard it said a few times. Or better still, avoid people who say that. I've even heard people mimic them – which makes my blood boil.

Avoid saying **"I've not paid to come on this ship to eat with the crew"** if you are lucky enough to share your table with an officer or the Captain. It's not big; it's certainly not clever and it's exceedingly old hat and boring.

What to avoid onshore…

Be wary of people who want to get too physically close. That woman with a clipboard asking you to sign a petition objecting to child poverty may not be as she seems. Once in Santa Cruz, Tenerife, I saw a young woman edge with a clipboard edge close to an elderly passenger who had just got off our ship. He tried to wave her away but as he was protesting, her hand was under the board relieving him of his wallet with all his cash and credit cards. I chased her but she vanished in a warren of alleyways. Luckily, there was a tourist office nearby and they helped to cancel his credit cards. A similar approach is used by beggars with babies.

Don't buy anything major off anyone selling on the street. They may show you a box with a nice shiny iPad or Camcorder at a knockdown price but it may either be stolen or they will switch the box when you're not looking. This happened to one of our waiters who thought he was buying a top of the range camera in Rome but when he opened the box, it contained 3 large oranges. Thereafter, his colleagues called him *Orange!* A costly way of getting your day's supply of Vitamin C.

Leave anything valuable in your safe. Don't be flashing a Rolex or a gold necklace about or you will be a target. Better still, leave it at home as your fellow passengers will probably think your expensive watch is a "Genuine Fake" seen in many ports ashore.

Always take the Port Guide provided for that particular day's port of call ashore with you. This is very important. If you get injured or miss the ship, it will have contact details of the cruise company's port agent who will be able to advise you what to do.

Beware of pedestrian crossings, especially in Europe. You may think you're safe but you will somehow seem invisible to motorists who will whiz past within inches. I had a lucky escape in Civitavecchia once where I was crossing the road after several cars stopped but a scooter rider totally ignored this and passed within centimetres of my toes!

In places like Rome and Florence you will be prosecuted and fined very heavily if the police catch you buying fake Gucci sunglasses or other fake designer goods. Just walk on by.

Don't fall for the old trick where someone "accidentally" squirts something on you and offers to wipe you down. While they are wiping, they will also be swiping.

Living statues will expect to be paid if you have your photograph taken with them and can get quite nasty sometimes if you fail to pay them. In Rome, for instance, avoid the "Gladiators" near the Coliseum. Sure they will let you have your picture taken with them but then they want a large amount of money for the pleasure and get threatening when you don't pay. They carry swords as well.

Don't stand in the middle of the pavement reading maps or guides. Do that in a less conspicuous spot.

Churches are a lucrative spot for pickpockets. Think about it. You put your bag down, kneel, close your eyes….

When using internet cafes, don't type in sensitive information such as bank account details. You can never know if the computer you are using has a keylogger which can record what you type and used to siphon your account.

TECHNOLOGY TRICKS AND TIPS

If you are reading this on a Kindle, tablet, computer or smartphone, the chances are you are already familiar with what's around in the field of technology and social media these days. It all helps when planning or managing your cruise, so here are a few ideas of how you can put it all to good use.

The most obvious is to prepare well in advance for your cruise by researching your ports of call on your computer. Make use of sites such as Cruise Critic and Trip Advisor to find out the highlights and lowlights; recommended restaurants, tourist traps and dangerous parts of the town or city to avoid. It will make your cruise run smoothly and save you a lot of time ashore.

Scan a copy of your passport and important documents into your computer and email them to yourself. You can then access them from anywhere in the world should the need arise. Also email emergency numbers such as the travel insurance claim line or your bank's helpline.

If you have an iPhone, iPad or similar, there are many apps specially designed for the cruising fraternity: Instead of carrying heavy guidebooks round the ports of call, download the digital guides provided by such companies as Dorling Kindersley; Rough Guides; Lonely Planet – and other independent developers. Saves space in the luggage too.

A translator app may come in handy if an emergency arises or if you need directions.

The "Ship Mate" series of apps covers most major cruise lines and covers such topics as :
- Real-time chat – meet those on your ship.
- Custom itinerary
- Ship & port info (with weather)
- Deck maps
- Cruise cameras

- Packing checklist
- Ship locator
- Excursion info
- Contact list
- Cruise tips
- Budget feature – keeping tabs on your onboard account.

Other useful items to download in advance include railway timetables; underground\metro maps and restaurant guides.

With an app such as Instapaper or Read Later, you can access information on your ports of call on your home computer, then save it to read offline while you're abroad.

If you spot something ashore you think is a bargain, don't impulse buy. Look for a wifi spot and check how much it costs back home to see if it actually *is* a bargain. Many shops put signs in their window when a particular ship arrives saying "Welcome ****** Passengers. Special 10% discount today" Take that with a pinch of salt.

If you don't want to carry a flashlight onboard, download a torch app, if you have an iPhone. It will light up the whole cabin.

You may also be able to download a Walkie-Talkie type app such as HeyTell which is just that. If someone else has the same app, no matter where in the world they are, you can find a free wifi connection ashore and talk to them at no cost. No costly phonecalls if you need to get a quick message across. You can also arrange to call them on Skype or Fring.

Internet access on your cruise is costly and may be frustratingly slow. Try and find a time when not many passengers are using it or you will end up paying for the slowness. I take a small netbook and compose my emails offline, then log on to send – thus saving very expensive long sessions typing online.

Turn off data roaming and voicemail before you sail or it could end up costing you a fortune. Beware connecting to the ships own telephone network as it will be very costly. Put in airplane mode if you don't need to make or accept calls.

Some reward schemes such as Princess's Captain's Circle include free internet time as part of the benefits.

Book tours cheaper online with reputable tour operators. Going off recommendations in various forums, we booked a full day's catamaran trip in Antigua and taxi tours of St Lucia and Grenada in advance and had a wonderful time seeing places off the beaten track.

Check online or on a weather app what the day's forecast is for your next port of call and you can dress appropriately.

If you see a member of the crew going off the ship with his laptop, follow him. You can bet that he knows where all the best free wifi hotspots are in port. He's probably been there dozens of times. Ask where the best reception is – they'll be happy to help.

QUEUEBUSTERS!

Do you enjoy queuing? You *may* do if you're British: after all, it is said to be a national pastime. On a cruise ship, you will have many opportunities to queue if that's your "thing".

If, on the other hand, you prefer to spend your time more profitably, here are some tips to avoid the dreaded standing in line…

The queues start forming outside the restaurants for dinner way before the stated opening time. You'll see maybe 100 cruisers in their posh frocks and natty jackets standing at the restaurant doors like runners on starting blocks. What is the point? You have been given a table at the start of the cruise. No-one is going to steal your place, so why queue along with the others who have also been allotted a table? Simply stroll down five or so minutes after "opening time" and you'll sail through the doors with a welcome *"Good Evening Sir and\or Madam"* and a pleasant smile from the Restaurant Manager and Maitre'd. Make your way to the table – you'll be in good time to order your meal and wine. Don't leave it any later though, or you'll be scowled at by your table companions: that is, if they have turned up on time

On embarkation, you can try turning up early but the only way to avoid the queues is to be granted priority embarkation and that only comes with moving up a few tiers of the rewards scheme.

The buffet area gets very busy at breakfast and lunchtime. Use the restaurant and the other dining options for a more relaxed meal.

If you are going ashore and want to make the most of it, order breakfast in your cabin for a quick getaway and to avoid queuing in the buffet or waiting to be served elsewhere.

Once, you achieve the higher echelons, if you get onboard and your cabin isn't ready, you will be taken to a place where free drinks and snacks will be available.

When in a port where it is necessary to go ashore by tender, there is more often than not a ticketing system in place. Usually, those who have booked tours are allowed off first, so it can be a long and frustrating wait until you are allowed onboard the tender to get to the port. The only thing to do in these circumstances is to get everything together you need to go ashore beforehand; have breakfast and make sure you pick up a ticket as soon as they are available. Your call time will be shorter as people tend to leave it later and they have to endure longer waits.

Some rewards schemes allow Priority Ship to Shore tender embarkation. If you're in the Elite Class of Princess Cruises Captain's Circle, for example, just flash your Elite cruise card at the tender embarkation area and breeze airily aboard. You won't have to wait with other passengers in the lounge area. What a feeling!
Be sure also to make a note of the time of the last tender back to the ship – *and avoid this at all costs.* The queues will be very long as people rush back to make it in time. Also, if you miss it, the ship won't wait for you to swim out to it. Aim to get to the tenders at least 30-45 minutes before the last one sails.

Another thing to make a note of is when the major tours are expected to arrive back either at the ship or back at the tender station ashore. If there are a dozen coaches full of passengers coming back at a certain time, you won't want to be stuck at the back of them – especially after a long hard day's sightseeing, drinking and eating in some hot clammy tourist trap.

If there is a **"chocoholics"** event or a galley tour (sometimes combined) on the ship, make sure you get there before the stated time. I guarantee there will be massive queues, sometimes half the length of the ship, formed by people dying to get their hands on the calorific comestibles.

A good time to grab a seat in a bar or lounge is about 30 minutes before the changeover between 1st and 2nd house shows. The ship will be at its quietest as 2nd sitting will be dining and most of the other passengers will be watching the first house performance.

Similarly, if there is a meet and greet with the Captain as well. Get there very early. Everyone wants to shake his hand. (Hope they wash them beforehand).

The worst queues onboard form at disembarkation. Sometimes the procedure is very efficient and at other times it can be slow and painful. This is because the luggage as to come off first and I suppose it may depend on how many other ships arrive at the same time. I remember being on a certain American liner once when it docked at Southampton and the disembarkation was so shambolic, it took hours. There weren't even any taxis in sight. The only way you can avoid this long wait is if you can manage to take off your own luggage. Let reception know and you will be given a priority pass to be among the first off. Passes are normally delivered to your cabin and allotted in different colours on the basis of furthest away, first off but if you're not travelling on a coach at a certain time, you can change these at reception if you are prepared to be naughty and tell a little white lie. (I couldn't possibly condone this). Otherwise, get to one of the lounges as soon as you can to get a comfy armchair or sofa; buy a newspaper and chill out. There's not a lot else you can do.

When you disembark, you will make your way to the baggage hall where (hopefully) your entire luggage will be waiting for you to carry through Customs. The trouble is, so will everyone else's. Quite frankly, it's a bit of a scrum with lots of people bumping into one another as they search the long lines of luggage which is sorted according to the deck you were on. It can sometimes take a while to find your items amongst all the thousands of others and the bigger the ship, the bigger the problem. Tempers sometimes get frayed and people panic when they imagine they can't see their luggage. (Sometimes, luggage is mislaid. It happened to a friend of ours who lost a suitcase which happened to be packed with boxes of cigarettes he'd bought ashore! Luckily, it was found later and forwarded to his home).

One solution is to make your luggage distinctive. If you don't fancy being seen with leopardskin suitcases or ones covered in pink polka dots, you can try the following before you put the cases outside your cabin for collection:

Tie a piece of coloured unusually patterned ribbon round the handle.

Wrap a piece of coloured Duck Tape round the case.

Buy some coloured Velcro Cable Ties and attach them to the handle in a loop.

Put some colourful stickers on it from a Card or Party Shop.

Trust me on this one. You'll be tired after your cruise and you may have a long journey ahead of you, so the last thing you'll want is to be engaged on a protracted suitcase hunt that takes the edge off your holiday.

Definitely make it distinctive!

CRUISE FREE!

Lots of people enjoy free cruises. They are the lecturers, after dinner speakers or people who specialize in teaching crafts such as card making, stuffed toys, flower arranging or pottery painting.
If you have a skill or a specialist knowledge of a subject, put it to good use and get those free holidays for yourself and a partner. Lots do!

REASONS TO CRUISE

You will have to decide what style of cruiser you are.

This will depend on (a) the amount you want to spend and (b) whether you are single, married, partnered, or with children.
Don't worry: everyone is catered for and I mean *everyone.*
Singles can book single cabins (at a premium, although sometimes they are available at the going rate). There are Singles' Meetups onboard and it isn't too hard to get chatting to other singles in the convivial atmosphere of a cruise ship, whether it be at dinner or on the dance floor.
Families can take advantage of the "kids go free" offers or the 3rd and 4th cabin occupancy discounts. The children have their own clubs, discos, eating places and scores of activities ranging from talent shows and games to artistic activities and games. It's common never to see your children for hours on end because they are enjoying themselves so much mixing with other kids of their own age and the Youth Team do a superb job in supervising and arranging activities.
There is even a baby-listening or babysitting service on many ships giving you the chance to have a well-earned break at dinner or a top class show.
Gay cruisers sometimes get the chance to meet others too when the "Friends of Dorothy" have special meetings in some cosy lounge – as do Masons, Rotarians and other special interest groups.
There are specific cruise lines for older passengers, notably Saga in the UK who only accept over 50's.

Longer cruises usually have older passengers because they are generally the ones who can afford them and have the time available. The 2 or 3 day ones generally suit the younger, boozier party crowd. Some ships even have alternative type Comedy Clubs where strong language is employed.

If you want to lounge by the pool without being assailed by noisy kids splashing and shouting, go on a child-free adults-only ship.

Your TA (Travel Agent) or an established guide such as the Berlitz Cruise Ship guide will advise.

Cruises aren't cheap – but they are also just as expensive as you want them to be.

You can book a Penthouse Suite with your own grand piano and butler costing a five figure sum, or you can bag a last-minute inside cabin at a fraction of the cost and sometimes half the price that the people in the cabin next door have paid.

The latter won't exactly make you popular with your fellow cruisers but as long as you don't walk round the decks wearing an *"I Paid Half What You Did"* tee shirt, who's to know?

Similarly with your onboard account: you can blow all your money on champers; fancy diamond rings and designer watches or you can by careful means, should you wish, end up paying nothing or next to nothing on your bill.

That's the beauty of cruising: it caters for all pockets – presuming you can afford a cruise in the first place.

The chances are you will be able to enjoy a cruise as more and more ships are being built to cater for this side of the holiday market, making it more affordable for people who many years ago would have been priced out of the equation.

You can book anything from a two or three-day "taster" cruise, right up to the World Cruise lasting anywhere over three months and taking a welcome chunk out of the Winter.

It is estimated over 12 million people a year go on a cruise. I reckon this means the cruise operators must be doing something right.

People say, once you've done your first cruise, you're hooked. That was certainly the case with our family. My wife Lynn, son Gareth and I have seen places we would never have seen if it hadn't been for cruising and met some wonderful people who we still regard as friends. It's probably one of the most relaxing ways to have a holiday.

Because:

There is no need for queuing at airports (unless you choose to fly out to join the ship).

You are waited on hand and foot by experts and the cost of all this can be less than £50 per person per night.

You don't have to peel spuds, cook or wash the dishes.

You can watch entertaining shows every night in theatres as good as West End ones – some with air-conditioned seats too.

The scenery changes constantly. One day you're in Venice…the next, Dubrovnik…

Your bed is made for you (and a little chocolate usually put on the pillow and sometimes a hand towel made into an item of origami).

You have many dining options and are guaranteed top-class cuisine. You can usually eat 24/7 too.

You can fill every minute of every day with the onboard and onshore activities.

If you have children, they are looked after for you – enabling you to get on with enjoying your holiday.

You can visit many different countries and capitals without having to drive there or work out an itinerary on public transport (and the hazards that involves).

The rewards schemes for frequent travellers are an added and very welcome bonus and usually start after your very first cruise. Take P & O for example. The previous Portunus Club scheme had three tiers, namely Ruby, Sapphire and Gold categories. The replacement Peninsular Club scheme has six distinct tiers: Atlantic, Pacific, Mediterranean, Caribbean, Baltic and Ligurian.

These are arranged in order of size with the most exclusive in the club being Ligurian.

The benefits of the various tiers are wide-ranging and include an on board discount varying from 5 to 10%; a free celebratory sailaway drink; discounted laundry; a clothes pressing service plus priority embarkation; travel insurance offer and early booking offers and priority cabin access.

In the replacement scheme, the top two tiers are exclusive to the most loyal passengers who have a total points value of more than 2500 - gained at 10 points per night spent onboard. Entry to these tiers is not only reliant on points but also requires a passenger to have spent over 80 nights on board any P&O Cruises ship within the three years prior to the start of their cruise.

Details are fully outlined on the P & O website.

You can travel safely alone and make friends and maybe meet that special person you've been looking for. Romance does happen on a cruise ship (they didn't call it the Love Boat for nothing).

To be honest, these are just some of the many reasons that make a cruise an ideal holiday. There are many more I can think of:

Watching schools of dolphins chase the ship; seeing the full moon reflected in the ocean on a balmy Mediterranean evening; witnessing the sun touch the horizon then rise back up again in the Arctic Circle; gliding through the indescribable majesty of the Fjords; sailing into the Grand Canal and watching Venice rise through the mist; steaming past the Statue of Liberty as New York greets the dawn – these are just some of the reasons that cruising becomes the addiction it undoubtedly is for people all over the world.

Happy Cruising and see you onboard!

Dave Dutton has many other ebooks on Amazon. Please do a search on the Amazon site for details of The Book of Famous Oddballs and Horrors! – and even more.

Printed in Great Britain
by Amazon